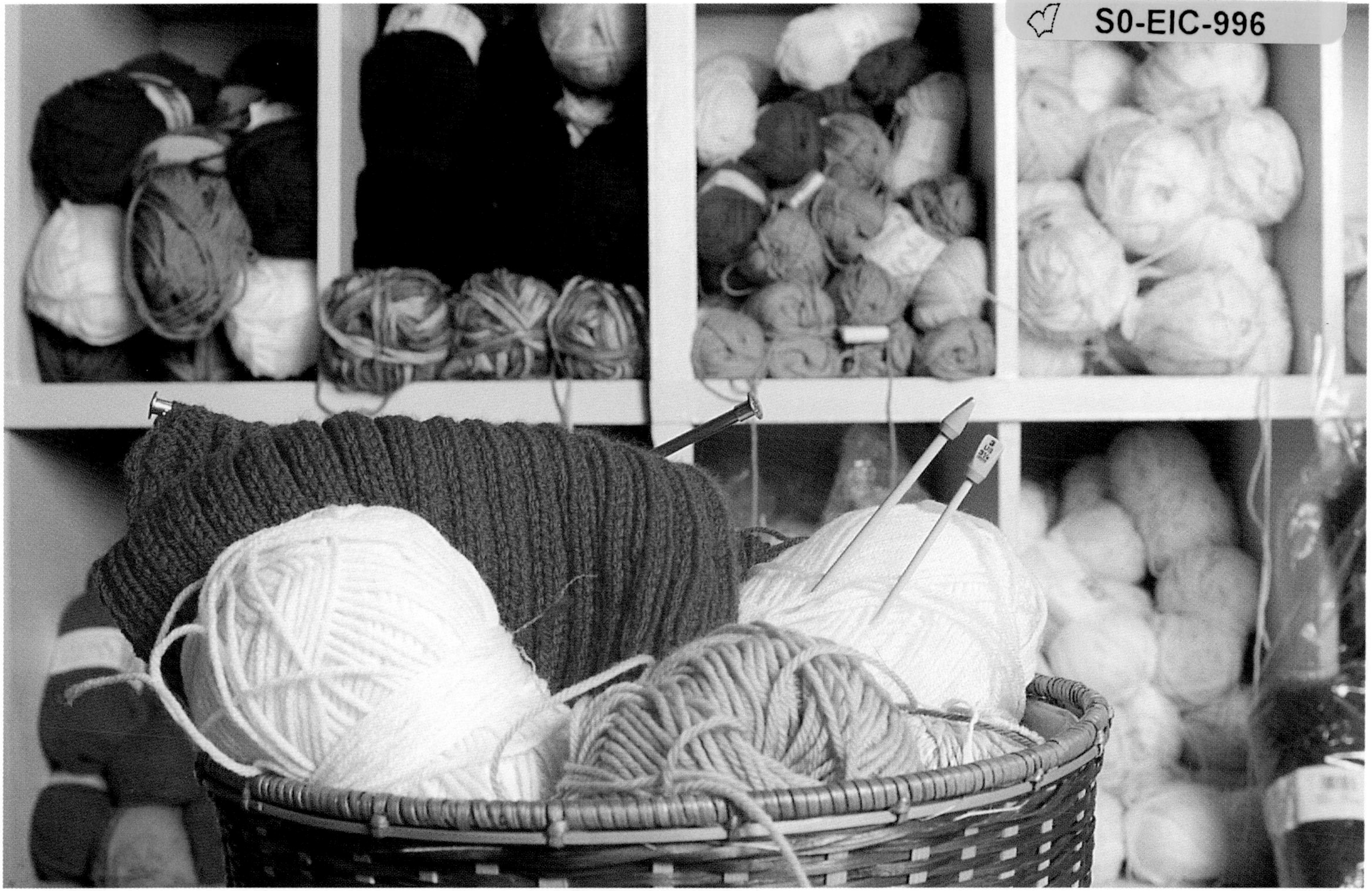

yarn

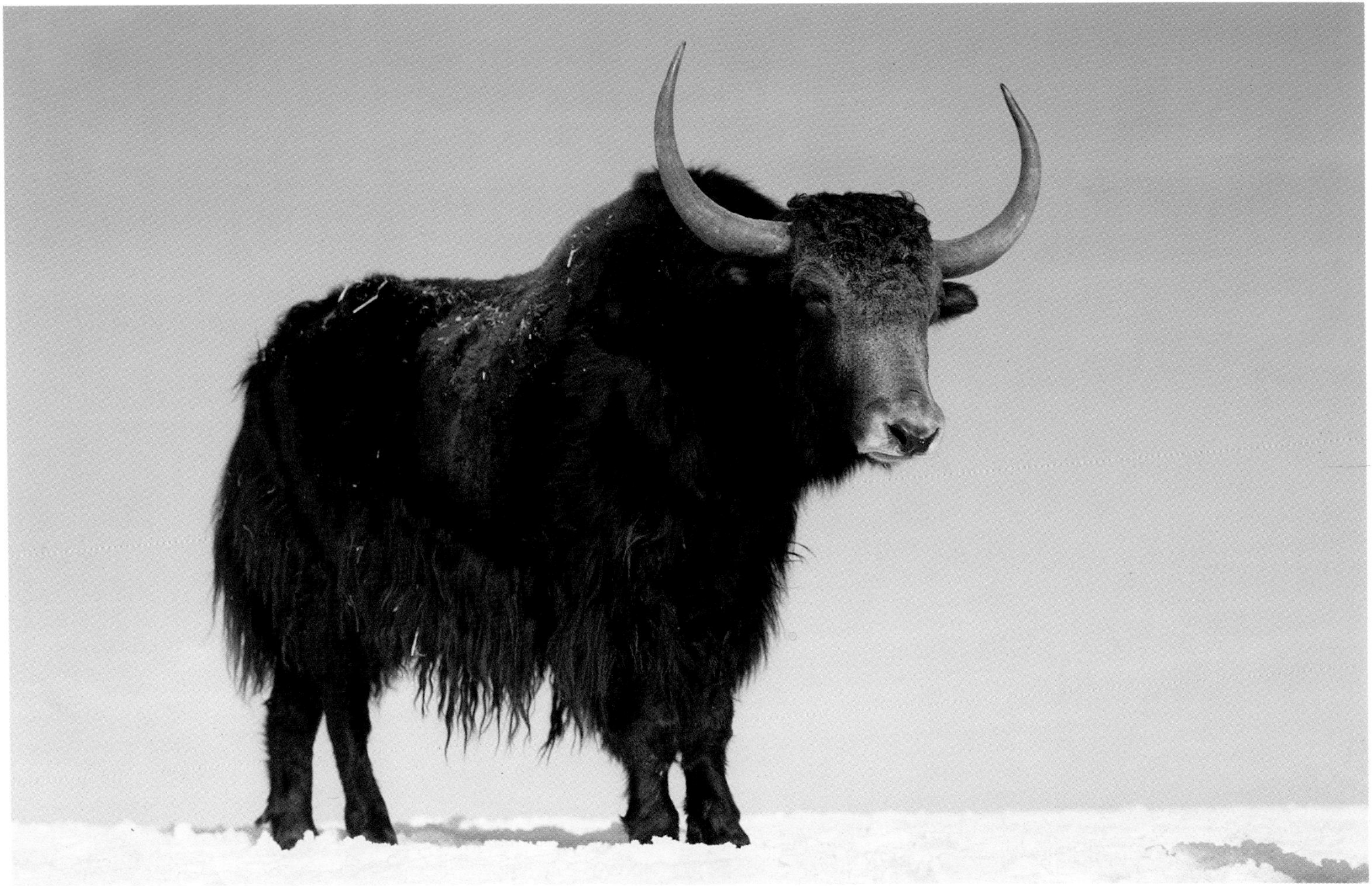

yak

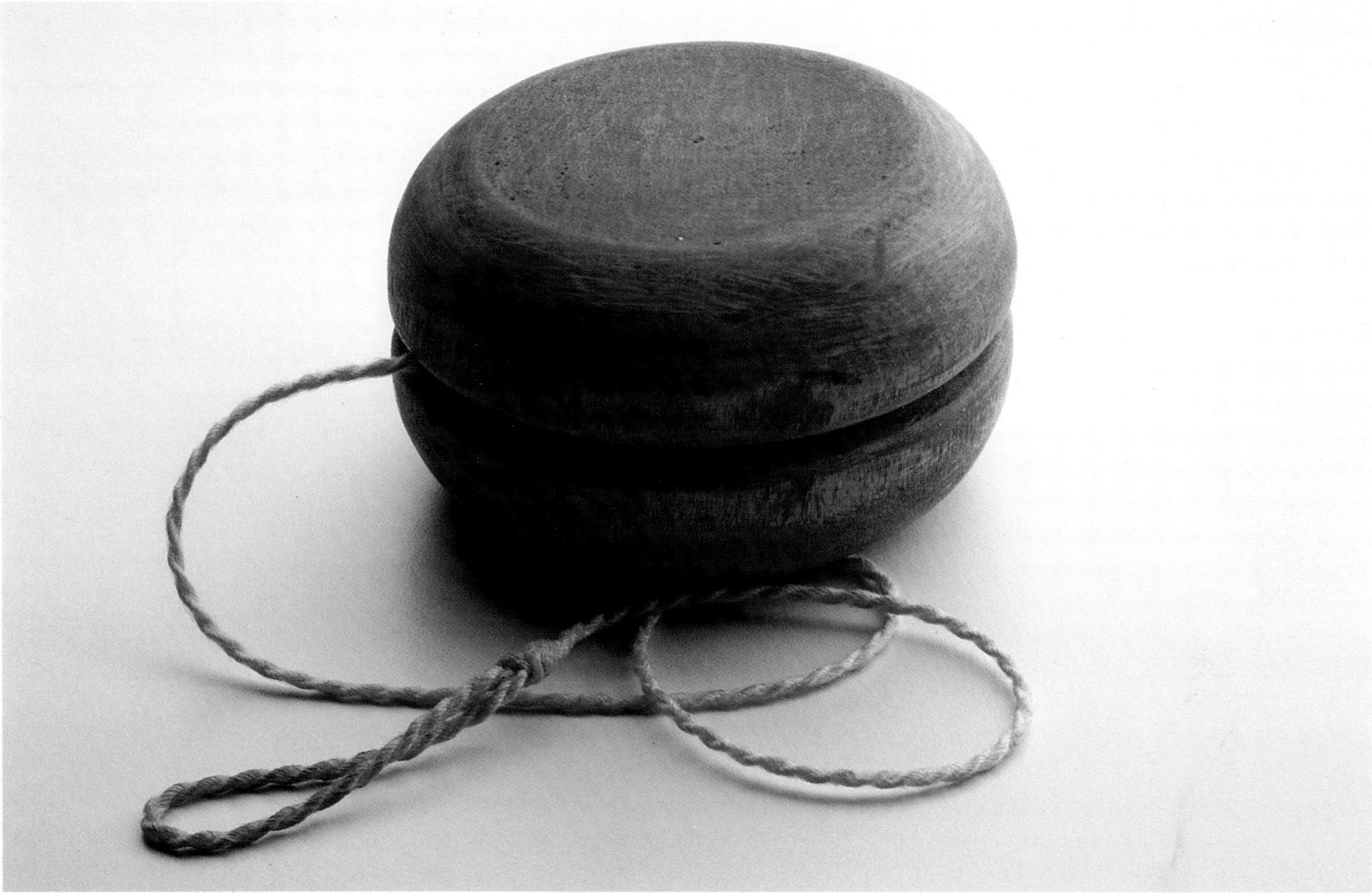

yo-yo

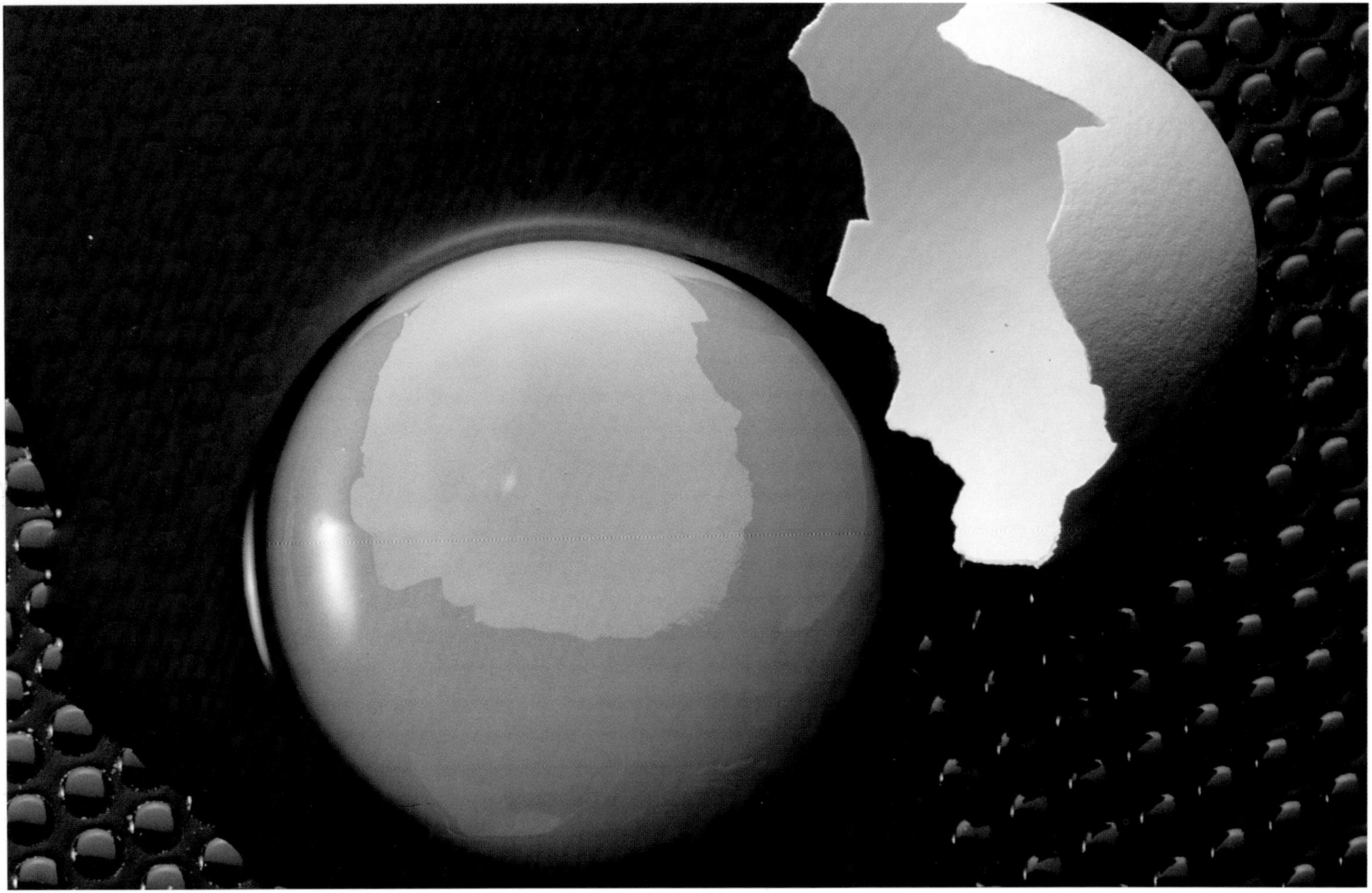

yolk

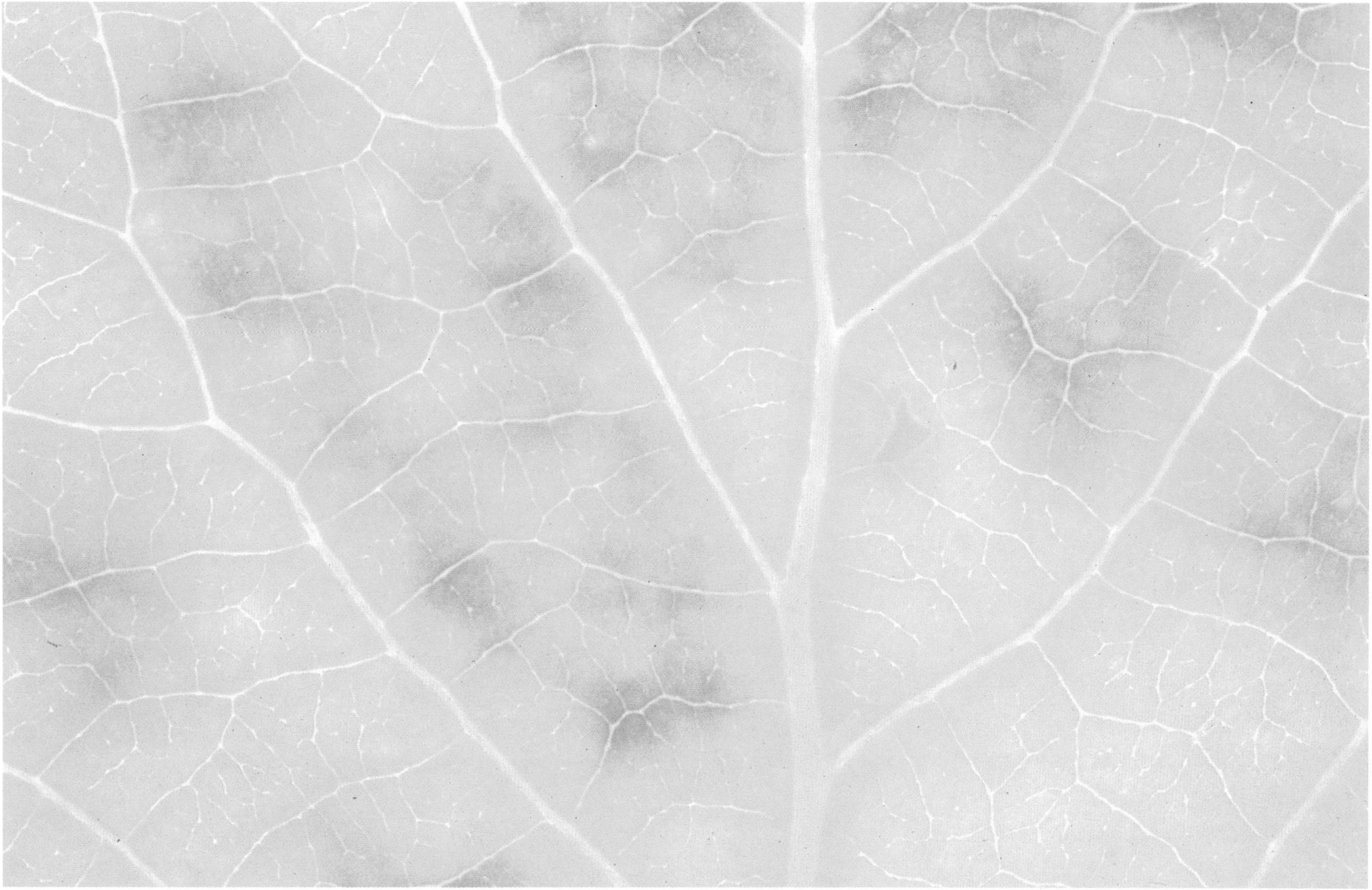

yellow

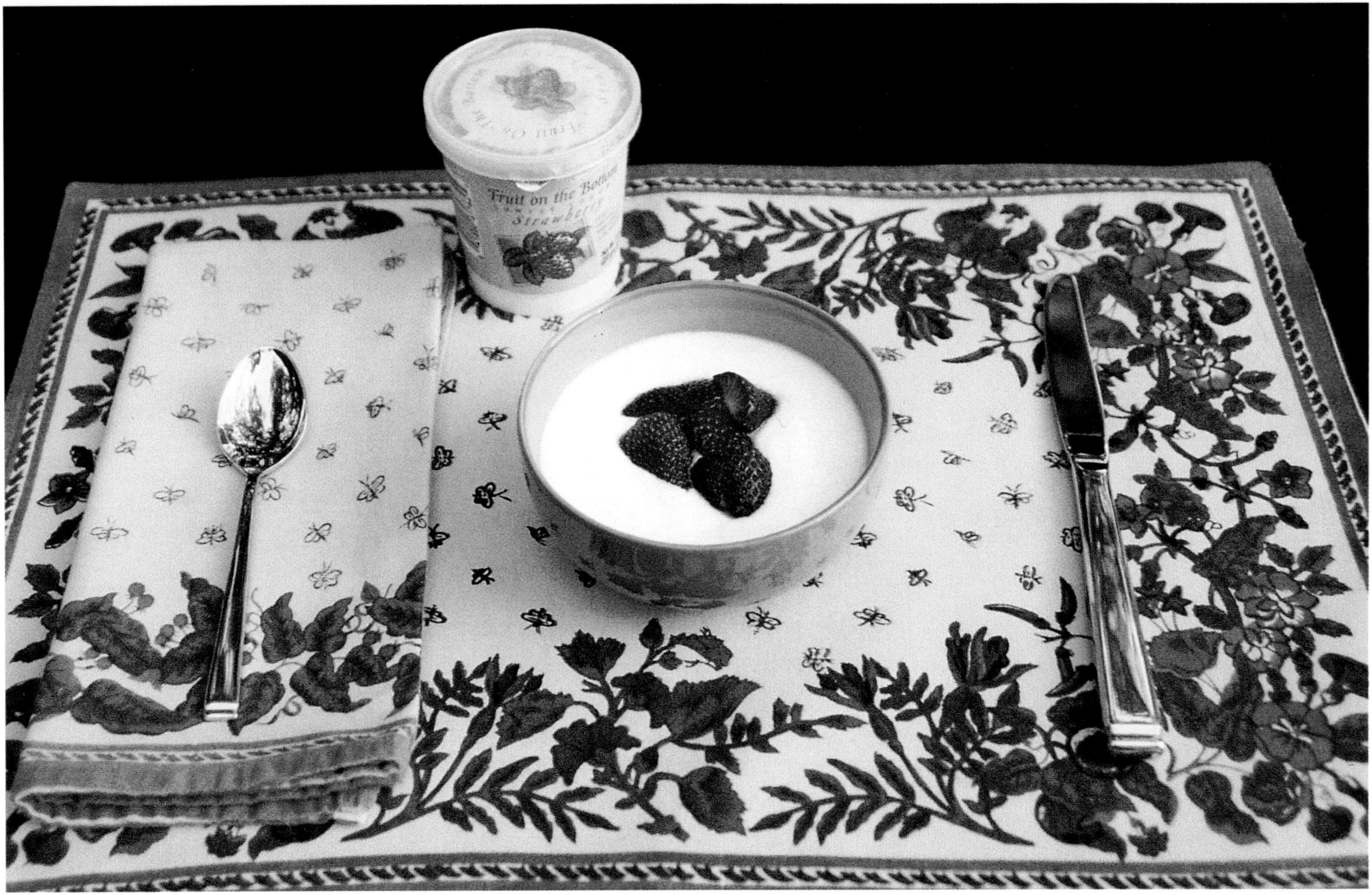

yogurt

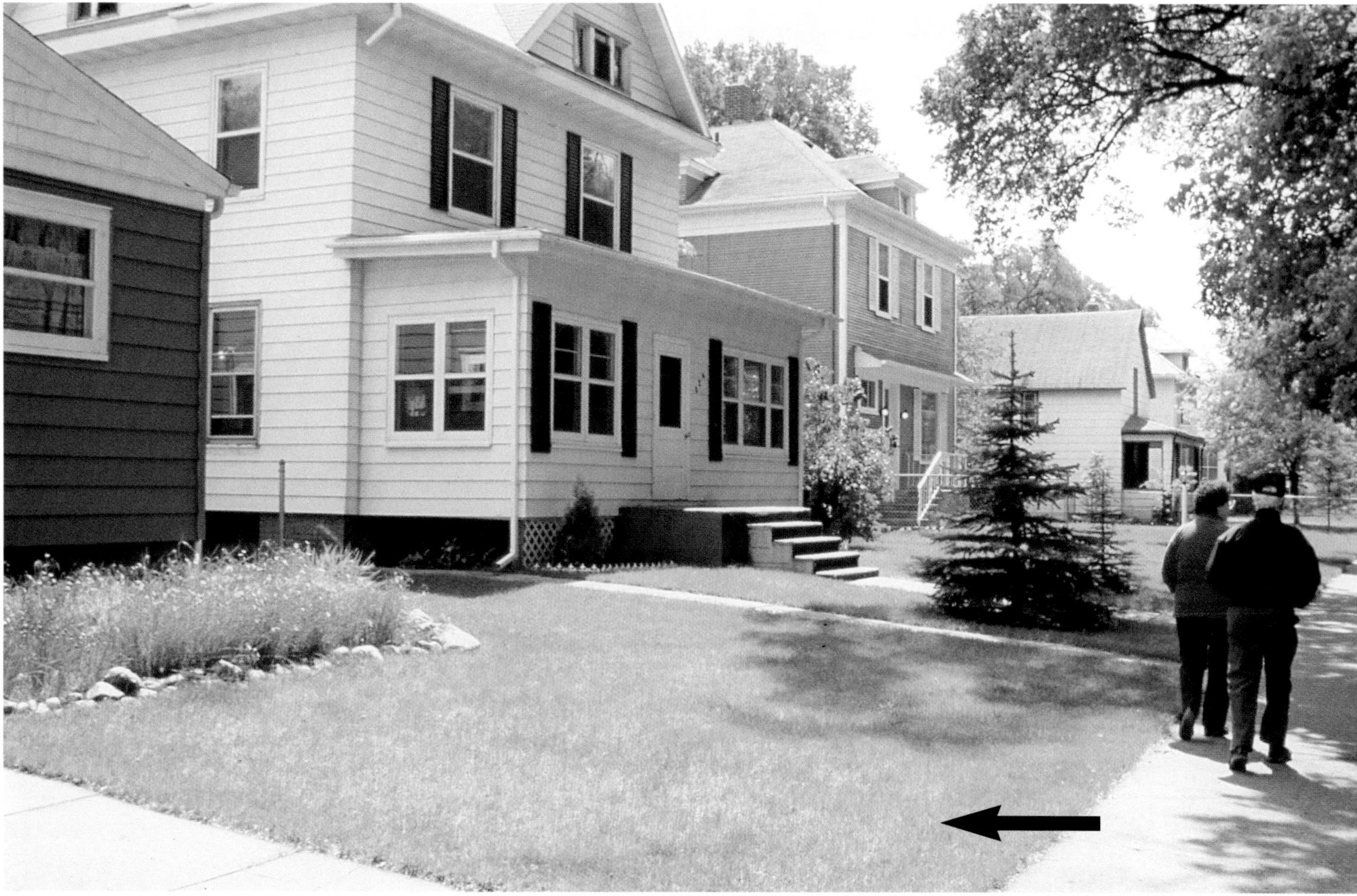

yard

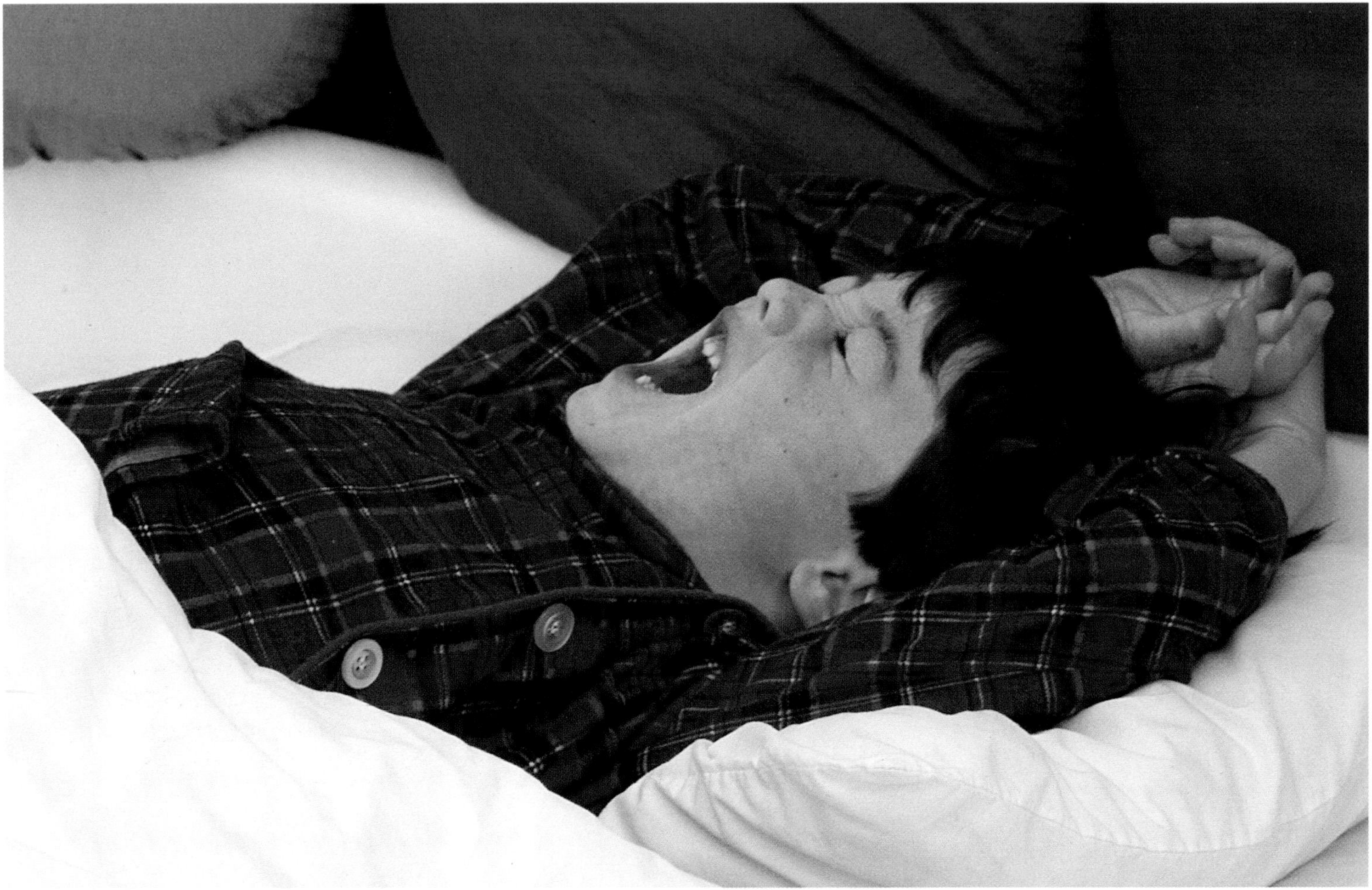

yawn